Books by Haki R. Madhubuti

Poetry

Run Toward Fear: New Poems and A Poet's Handbook

Heartlove: Wedding and Love Poems

Ground Work: New and Selected Poems of Don L. Lee/Haki R. Madhubuti
    from 1966-1996

Killing Memory, Seeking Ancestors

Earthquakes and Sunrise Missions

Book of Life

Directionscore: New and Selected Poems

We Walk the Ways of the New World

Don't Cry, Scream

Black Pride

Think Black

Non-Fiction

Tough Notes: A Healing Call for Creating Exceptional Black Men

Claiming Earth: Race Rage Rape, Redemption:
    Blacks Seeking a Culture of Enlightened Empowerment

Dynamite Voices: Black Poets of the 1960s

Black Men: Obsolete, Single, Dangerous? The Afrikan
    American Family in Transition

From Plan to Planet: Life Studies; The Need for Afrikan Minds and
    Institutions

Enemies: The Clash of Nations

A Capsule Course in Black Poetry (co-author)

African Centered Education (co-author)

Anthologies

Releasing the Spirit: A Collection of Literary Works from
    Gallery 37 (co-editor)

Describe the Moment: A Collection of Literary Works from
    Gallery 37 (co-editor)

Million Man March/Day of Absence: A Commemorative
    Anthology (co-editor)

Confusion by any Other Name: Essays Exploring the Negative Impact of
    The Black Man's Guide to Understanding the Black Woman (editor)

Why L.A. Happened: Implications of the "92 Los Angeles
    Rebellion (editor)

Say that the River Turns: The Impact of Gwendolyn Brooks (editor)

To Gwen, With Love (co-editor)

Run Toward Fear

New Poems And
A Poet's Handbook

Haki R. Madhubuti

Third World Press
Chicago
2004

Third World Press
Publishers since 1967

First Edition 2004
Printed in the United States of America
Printed by R.R. Donnelley

10 09 08 07 06 05 04   8 7 6 5 4 3 2 1

Library of Congress Cataloging-in-Publication Data

Madhubuti, Haki R., 1942-
    Run toward fear : new poems and a poet's handbook /
Haki R. Madhubuti.
        p. cm.
    ISBN 0-88378-260-X (cloth : alk. paper)
    ISBN 0-88378-265-0 (pbk. : alk. paper)
    1. African Americans—Poetry. 2. World politics—Poetry. I.
Title.

PS3563.A3397R86 2004
811'.54—dc22   2004047968

Cover art by Theodore A. Harris , "On the Heel of Famine" © 1998
    A collage based on a line from a poem by Tony Medina.
Layout and design: Nicole M. Mitchell
Author photo: Lynda Koolish

Some of the poems in this collection have been previously published
and have appeared in *Tough Notes: A Healing Call for Creating
Exceptional Black Men*, *Chicago Sun Times*, *Black Issues in Higher
Education*, *Chicago Tribune*, *N'digo*, *Brilliant Corners*, and the "Poetry
Center's Limited Edition Letterpress Broadside"

For the Dedicated
Lives and Work of

Ruby Dee and Ossie Davis,
Beverly and Walter P. Lomax Jr.,
Arundhati Roy,
Bob Herbert,
Murry DePillars,
Claud Anderson,

and for
Young people of all nations
the real hope
for the world.

In Memory of

Gwendolyn Brooks
Tom Feelings
Jeff R. Donaldson
Malachi Favors
Jacob H. Carruthers
Jaramogi Abebe Agyman
Kevani Zelpah Moyo
Beah Richards

And
All the young people
Who lost their lives in our country's
Misadventures in Iraq

Contents

III

Art hurts. Art urges voyages.
        Gwendolyn Brooks

*You are what you do
beyond any saying of it.*
        Keorapetse Kgositsile

*Every artist / a burglar.
Who / steal from tradition.*
        Sterling D. Plumpp

*What do you want, America?
Young bearded nation of the thick muscles
that does not sleep
against the breasts of past greatness
what do you want, America?*
        Frank Marshall Davis

*In America, you can segregate the people,
but the problems will travel.*
        June Jordan

Fear

It is the poets who run toward fear.
They are what we read,
think and speak,
fighting for greater possibilities
than the words of tabloids and broadsheets where
Texas and London compare notes as
cries of 9/11 loudly emerge out of context
connected to dust on the throats of
authority and might disguised
as camouflaged revenge in the night
from small heads of an imperial
news speak.
back page the greed of Enron, WorldCom
and Halliburton. clustered
vampires needing fresh blood
rally against a mosquito whose flesh
is dark and oily, slippery and deadly
as our homeland colors are manipulated
between yellow, orange, red and re-election.

I

In Another Land

their parents' eyes no longer glow
they are water full and deplete
anchoring horror and hunger scarred faces.
children weighted down with loss of families, friends,
trust, homes, land, work, local scent, livestock,
dignity and a country where indigenous schools
fail to prepare them for refugee status
or quick exits with grandmothers in wheelbarrows and
pregnant women driving tractors on one-way roads.

Kosovo is like Rwanda, Bosnia, and other recent histories,
small men with guns and putrid ideas
spit in the face of sanity, reason and why.
today's leaders stand before maps and spin lies
as televised and tortured children
wade through natural and man made mud
while quietly praying for bread, meat, blankets,
revenge and clean water, with only their
questioning minds and culture,
empty stomachs and warm hands,
shattered doubts, history and dreams.

this is how new hatred is created
how centuries of ugly
memories are introduced to pre-teens and babies
whose smiles have disappeared or are broken
frozen in the tears of parents and elders who
whisper of a future, of possibilities
in the privacy and temporary protection of donated tents.

Remembering the children of Kosovo

Legal Lottery

the only men i saw
reading the starr report
on president clinton were lawyers.
they were not reading for facts on whitewater,
travelgate or sexual insight on the use of cigars.
they weren't necessarily interested in impeachable crimes.
they read each word
of every sentence of every paragraph
looking for, eagerly in search of,
the secrets to a fifty million dollar payday.

Chicago is Illinois Country

we are the breast and chest of this nation,
four seasons on the shores of hope
where ideas and fresh water feed
hearts and land in this century's city,
all aware that we can be illumination,
velocity, bread, breath and motion.

we, the carriers of deep earth, sun, snow, desert
and red clay, collided in search of soul and finality.

there are recent padlocks on our memories.
neither infidels or unbelievers   we are loosely
camouflaged and choreographed dancers.
out of necessity and accelerated foresight,
we arrived as unsettled bones and motion.

calm   we are not
satisfied   we are not

our music is the accretion of
multiple tongues into one language
the indomitable spirit harmonizing in
must do theaters where second as in city or state
is absent from our vocabulary and intentions.

we, carriers of all cultures,
invented untried futures
gathered the sane vitality of distant spheres
to narrate an illuminated vision and motion
in this city,
in this state,
in the breast and chest of this nation.

Illinois Humanities Council establishes the
Studs Terkel Humanities Service Award, November 6, 2002

Art

1

Art is a prodigious and primary energy force. Children's active participation in music, dance, painting, poetry, film, photography and the indigenous crafts of their people is what makes them whole, significantly human, secure in their own skin, culture and abilities. Thus, generating in them unlimited possibilities.

Art is fundamental instruction and food for a people's soul as they translate the many languages and acts of becoming, often telling them in no uncertain terms that all humans are not pure or perfect. However, the children of all cultures inherit their creators' capacity to originate from the bone of their imaginations the closest manifestations of purity, perfection and beauty. Art at its best encourages us to walk on water, dance on top of trees and skip from star to star without being able to swim, keep a beat or fly. A child's "on fire" imagination is the one universal prerequisite for becoming an artist.

2

Magnify your children's mind with art,
jumpstart their questions with art,
introduce your children to the cultures of the world
through art,
energize their young feet, spirits and souls with art,
infuse the values important to civil culture via art,
keep them curious, political and creative with art,
speak and define the universal language of
beauty with art,
learn to appreciate peace with art,
approach the cultures of others through their art,
introduce the spiritual paths of other
people through their art.
keep young people in school, off drugs and

out of prison with art,
keep their young minds running, jumping
and excited with art.
examine the nurturing moments of love,
peace and connecting differences with art

3

Art allows and encourages the love of self and others. The best
artists are not mass murderers, criminals or child molesters;
they are in the beauty and creation business. Art is elemental
to intelligent intelligence, working democracy, freedom, equality
and justice. Art, if used wisely and widely, early and often,
is an answer and a question. It is the cultural lake that the
indigenous rivers of dance, music, local images and voices
flow. Art is the waterfall of life, reflecting the untimely and
unique soul of a people. Art is the drumbeat of good and great
hearts forever seeking peace and a grand future for all
enlightened peoples. For these are the people the world over
who lovingly proclaim, "give the artist some," kind words,
financial support, yeses from your heart, knowing intuitively
that there will be creative reciprocity in all that they give us.
Why? Because fundamentally art inspires, informs, directs,
generates hope and challenges the receiver to respond.
And finally, and this is consequential, the quality of the art
determines the quality of the responses.

What Do You Say?

replacing fools and crooks
with other fools and crooks
is to the democratic legislative process
what salt is to the seasoning
of over cooked neck bones.
they both kill.

Wasted Life

he spent fifty years
of his life
trying to convince
white people that
he was as good as they were.
he not only failed
but
didn't learn anything
from the experience except
to strategically forget his name and
lie in long sentences.

We Need Not Whisper

We need not whisper
this to neighbors or friends.
We need not kneel or hide our emotions
at this hour.
We need not fail to call up the history of Black flight
caught between success, BET and the
color of gold and coal.
We need not shuffle or polka
to accordion music in 6/8 time.
We need not cry or grin in silence
as white bullets rip the spine, split the brain and
shatter the dreams and lives of our children.

We have new definitions.
We are the offspring of Chaka Zulu, Nat Turner,
Ida. B. Wells, Duke Ellington, Paul Robeson, Rosa Parks,
Martin Luther King, Malcolm X, Ella Baker, Harold Washington,
Gwendolyn Brooks, gospel and blues.
We are not new Negroes reacting to the rap of
unsmiling and misguided sons and daughters modeling
over priced starter jackets for the GAP, Wall Street and MTV.
We are bright definitions and
accepting quietly the murder of our children
is not one of them.

In memory of Amadou Diallo, Tyisha Miller and others

Gate Keepers

the seeing is in the listening
it is where you walk and sleep that matters
it is the Black and why in the question that demands answers,
it is the done deal before the critique.
gate keepers run from moments to tell
truth to children or power,
truth they deem better if delivered
in anthropological language
that caused their mommas
to apologize to God and family for
sending their only child to Harvard
to be educated and to find himself.

Missed Information

too many people say
they in love
with each other
they cars,
they houses, they churches,
they finger nails laced with diamonds,
they love oprah & montel & pig feet
eaten in secret because it ain't cool
to eat the feet of pigs in public
especially by those who wear tailor-made dresses and pin-
stripe suits.
they say love makes them do it
love is the "o" and "y" as in only you
which is believable if you are 14
and separated from your mind and soul
which is a legal excuse if you were
educated in the public schools of houston, detroit, chicago or
new york.
"I love you" the famous last words of
tom's uncle bobo to lincoln just before
he took back they 40 acres and a mule,
condoleezza, bobo, bertha and colin are in love,
they proud too.
that's another story.

Laws of the Street

if someone among the men
assemble on the corner of 47th & ellis
in front of bj's bar,
all talking shit and spit,
looks like he wants to attack
you
it is best to fire on him first
with the fury and force of a thousand guerrillas
not to just knock him down
but to firmly plant in his mind
hard reasons
for not getting up.

Can You Write a Non-Struggle Poem?

Can you write a poem not about politics, culture, economic
struggle or the possibilities of drinking unfiltered water?
Can you put words of rhythm together that do not comment on
the warmth and cold of indigenous teas and corporate coffee or
the conflict of words, worlds and actual life? Is it possible to
render musical language into the yin and yang of acupuncture
healing points, the yeses, nos, and questions of accepted
thought, the rich and poor of potatoes, bean and rice eaters
without surveying landscapes of corrupted lifestyles and
hideouts of platinum credit card holders? Must your poems
always remind us of tortured citizens, the nation's homeless,
urban schools and assembly line workers? Why write about
million dollar condo owners and the culture of food stamp
users in the same line? Is not the economic divide between
women and men a known quantity, and what of the super egos
of politicians, public intellectuals and medical doctors rendered
in free verse? Is not the arrogance of America's imperialism,
the elitism of professors misusing language and ideas
expected, just as that of preachers, priests, rabbis, monks and
imams interpreting the world of God unquestionable and
naturally poetic? What of the aloneness and fear of children
dancing between broken families, state and private agencies
looking for clean love and healing human touch as subject
matter for serious poets? It would truly take a master poet to
link tax loopholes of the rich with the wars over oil, water, dark
earth, neck-bone eaters and the F.C.C. giveaways. Poetry, we
are told, doesn't play well in the company of the military and
prison industrial complexes or that of retired generals quickly
joining the executive work forces of Boeing and General
Electric. You forget that poets are not lobbyists, or
ambassadors for reason. They are dreamers and talkers and
love chasers. They need to concentrate on reading and writing
poetry and let the professionals continue to mismanage words,
the world and wonderment.

II

Amiri

baraka
"always
come in a
      place
later."
rushin to catch words that came before him
tho that don't much matter,
him got his own words, music, dance, dramatics
& bright ideas even if some of them used cars
& don't work.   but baraka works
works harder than 15 men his age,
da, da da, do   who been around
long enough to tell his time
in places where people have tried to
beat the beat & tempo out of his talk & walk.
monk, trane & duke played secrets
that saved him & us even if we didn't
accurately hear their da da, doos
baraka did. they spoke musically to him.
he gave us his many languages & genius.
his comin in time is getting better & best & less late,
even for this sage still makin up stories
actin on his own stage & firing truthpoems
that compel liars & politicians to exit early & often.

For Amiri Baraka

17

Baraka II

i saw *The Dead Lecturer* in a Chicago airport.
pacing, fast walking probably quick thinking about
unfinished projects like plays, poems and essays about
"successful" negroes supporting Bush & Ghost
and the secrets of whites with rhythm and
mass graves in Rwanda;
mostly *Tales* of *The System of Dante's Hell* out of school
really way past graduate courses taught
on the rough-neck streets
of Newark. A kind of *Funk Lore* in 3/4 time.
recently, i saw *Black Fire, In Our Terribleness* – older and
small but still a witness with missing teeth, grayer hair with a
fast smile in a blue shirt, accentuated by a smokin Egyptian
print tie – on the south side of Chicago.
Spirit Reach with his *Hard Facts* was alone and
standing close to a pay phone without an assistant,
credit or debit cards, without lovers of literature or *Jello*
supporting him. No *Kawaida Studies* here.
his aloneness frightens me, approaching him I wondered
why this genius of serious music,
of transcendent literature wasn't
surrounded by readers, fans, collectors of fine words on pages
seeking instructions and autographs.
It's Nation Time is still asleep.
where were the *Blues People* and *Black Magic* folks?
S.O.S. for the *Slave* ships and *The Motion of History* souls.
where were the consumers of best sellers, few sellers & the
new line of negro confessional booty-call stores. maybe
they just didn't notice this *Wise, Why's, Y's* poet,
this lover of language, passionate protector of
sound and the laughter of children.
maybe they were blinded by their bones of contradiction –
and pimp juice traversing their veins. they looked past this
original and complicated seer of Black life, this *The Moderns*
updated, reworked beyond *Transbluesency*,
there will be no *Eulogies* here,

no *Preface to a Twenty Volume Suicide Note*,
just an older and able African son going *Home*,
pacing the floor at Midway Airport
on the southside of Chicago, thinking and
alone with a swift – smile.
"whats happenin bro?"

Baraka III

It's difficult to be talented
& genius
yet, often called crazy to your face
in a place that rewards moneymakers
who build and worship skyscrapers as monuments
to the individuality of dollar
bill collecting and preemptive war making
& whose poets and artists are viewed
as handicapped, a bit mad with water colored hands & ideas.
artists who work at beauty, wear words
bathed in nature & music,
talk in complex sentences, odd metaphors & swinging
feet are confusing to themselves and others.
they also think too much about
the nature of flags and forests,
the truth of institutions & religions
of language and lawyers, bankers & brokers;
the why & who of homelessness,
the question of collateral damage and
the battle between cultures, races & classes out of school.

actually, being a complete artist
in a place that worships skyscrapers, money, war,
misconceived thought and hummer2 over children
requires a bit of madness.

Why Shani?

Old folks say that the most
courageous and committed people
are tested incessantly,
given the most intricate mountain to forge,
the deepest forest fires to quiet,
the harsher hellholes to navigate.
this journey does not inspire struggle
just unlimited offers of another path
to reconsider opposing injustice,
to stop working for the children of strangers,
to cease cleaning the wounds of the battered,
to abandon poetry.

to rise from unanswerable pain
requires a history beyond the acquisition of things,
demands work on the other side of self and self.
you have labored and researched the catalogs of the world
& refused to be separated from the poor and poorer.

your love for us is uncorrupted and contagious,
grounded in your arts, activism and the familial.
we reciprocate.

For the Baraka Family

Remembering Betty Shabazz

i, a poet, a weaver of life, an unfinished soul in motion   still
a closet dancer who greyhounded between
detroit and chicago
on the same roads
that Malcolm Little, Malcolm X, El Hajj Malik El Shabazz
traveled the identical highways
that Betty, Betty Shabazz, Dr. Betty Shabazz questioned   still
i, a poet, an observer of life, met Betty,
giver and nurturer of black winds and earth,
airborne at 33,000 feet over pennsylvania in the year of 75

i, a poet whose voice was confirmed, layered & enlarged
    after hearing
a "young shining prince," before we knew
we had the sons of kings and queens among us whispering
African truths that gutted the whiteness in our bellies & minds

i, a poet with watered eyes proclaimed cultural love for black
    memory, future,
family and to Betty Shabazz: a genuine work
in progress devoted to
six plus more of her blood and bones.   still

i, a poet, a weaver of life's tales, found a gift at 33,000 feet
a stand for something spirit in st. john knits, sipping vernon's
    ginger ale
a soul in motion electric sliding to the music
of "I'm every woman...
it's all in me," forever observant of predators selling sister love,
    baby love
and a woman's place, a woman's place.   still

i met a woman not a victim,
i met a sister not a tragedy
i met a warrior-teacher not a professional widow,
i met a baobab tree standing permanently against
human hurricanes & earthquakes   still
she was city and voice and insightful storm,
a drop-dead shopper only to give most away,
viewed young people as possibilities, psychic nourishment,
undeveloped innocence mother thoughts   still
she had grown into gianthood
did not fear nameless faces anymore
her prayerful language accented
"hey, girlfriend" or "my brother" burns in our memories   still
peace be still, dear Betty
who found the good in us and praised it
I'm every woman, woman, woman,
it's all in me   still.

For Maya Angelou, Ruby Dee, Laura Ross Brown,
and Susan L. Taylor

Bones

she riffs in less than fifty words
poems that unveil a peoples' bones.

improvising veto-proof likeness
she cleans neighborhoods of celebrated ignorance
among the weak, wicked and wise,
among the wounded, weary and brief winners.

with oxygen lines,
with a vernacular voice and memory
she sings, swims and dances to the merry movements
of the underlooked, bloodflow, heartdrums
and blistered feet of betrayed generations.

this museum of a poet is not about
impressing enemies, friends or lovers,
her urges are to write gladness, grief and melodies,
always probing for trustworthy tales
of her deep-south multitudes.   acutely
aware of the exaggerations of politicians,
public intellectuals and the criminally rich
she is our brilliant testifier.

For Lucille Clifton

A Mixture of Rain, Rice and Silence

men seldom reveal their hearts to other men
you are listener and conscious galaxy
not quite stone
more like pieces of a royal mountain
where flowers, rainbows, memory and rich earth integrate.
your singing and dancing made me
look like an original member of the Temptations.
yet,
you are a mixture of rain, rice and silence,
one who practices faith, breathes truth and labors
confirming that a moral life is not a dull life for
a basketball player who is gentle with children and
the broken hearts of the wounded forgotten.
they say you love your people,
they say you are authentic and rare,
they say you are calm and storm and love the law,
like Marvin Gaye I call you brother, brother
infinitely more than a footnote
much like a carefully worded
prose poem searching for our collective hearts.

For David Hall at Fifty
May 26, 2000

The Journey

the missed steps are the most frightening
the unsureness of the calling
wondering if there will be
a hand, a will, a way, a plan
yes, a people
who understand the almost
impregnable face of whiteness
in all of its veiled and public permutations.

if Black people are America's hopeful metaphor
imagine for a moment, just a moment,
the utter responsibility of Black Leadership,
officers without a focused army,
ill equipped for the details of polluted speech,
deciphering small print, questionable deal making,
disguised remunerations, an adulterous culture and
objectionable amendments to Democracy.

statesmen and women who seem stateless
struggle over Black bones,
              Black memory,
              Black hope and promises
              Black conscience, territory and integrity.
herein is the journey
be not broken words, deeds or
stale flowers on unmarked graves.
claim justice,
demand vigilance of courts and kindergartens,
resist evil in all colors and configurations,
do not fear truth, criticism or Black love.
speak knowledge.
do not whisper in the ears of enemies,
because of elaborate egos, attitudes and corruption.
betrayal is an easy door at noon or midnight,
rejecting corporate bounty is the backbone exam.

speak courage forcefully
remember you are our fire and water,
                our light and wind,
                our voice and answer,
                our agent of warmth, wisdom and sun.
you are our language, spirit and definitions.

love is where we emerged,
love is where we will travel,
love is at the pilgrimage end,
is the reality guiding your work.
the reason we negotiate mountains and persevere.

run like lions on the hunt,
others think that they know us.
that too is our ace, our secret, our bond.
leadership may only last a season
let the rain come,
we are the earth.

For the Congressional Black Caucus Thirtieth Anniversary
Celebrations, September 2001

We Family

We family,
we friends,
we neighbors,
we assemblage of smiling folk
mostly strangers at this gate
gathered south to confirm
this cornerstone of cultures,
this joining of names and spirits,
this remarkable sharing of water
deep breathing, gold, grandmother tales,
bread, music, cloth, life's fragments and genuine love.

Your fathers are pleased and joyous,
your mothers are tearful and earthful,
those gathered are thankful,
all are concerned and most earnest in their
good words, well wishes, exact advice and gifts.
the flowers are happy, the air invigorating
today's passion is meditative and prayerful.

This sacred ritual of ocean crossing,
of consenting hearts, families and traditions
is the blessing
is too a warning, hot soup, sweet pastry, green cultivation,
lusted waterfalls, untamed climate, quiet talk, unknown steps,
complex hours, birth,
yams, bold darkness, abundant wellness and histories.
this clasping of hands,
this smiling silence,
this rooted journey of two African souls
has spirited us home this day.

Our extended stillness and thoughts
second these original lovers
who are prompt and prepared,
suitable and equipped for life's arrangements & traditions.

Of those here gathered
we urgently assert and affirm that
we be family,   now and now
unremittingly.

For Janet Danielle Hutchinson and Bomani Garvey Madhubuti Lee,
married on September 15, 2001 and for the Hutchinson
and Madhubuti families.

Our Daughter On Loan

you were not to be ours forever,
yours was a short map.
some say a liberian circle
there is little human logic to your pilgrimage.
we must not deem it incomplete,
we do confirm that it was brief.

the day the sun bloodied,
the moon disappeared,
interrupting great promise and progress,
magnificent expectations.
visual artists painted muted yellows,
poets and musicians were silent and
fiction writers and dancers joined hands and tears
the second your breath stopped.

your history was still in discovery
as grandmothers, big mommas and babas declared,
"you were on loan to us,"
not a borrowed book or pawn shop watch.
your visit among us is still mystery and melody,
"tweety" birds with rhythm in their eyes.

your mother is a southern river,
your father a strong stone with baggage,
your family is Black stories, deep crops,
gathering winds, Black hurricanes in waiting.
you were washed in love and possibilities,
sun bathed in smiles, tunes and cultural signatures.
why you leave us so soon?

For Kevani Zelpah Moyo
(1982-1999)

Black Earth

she was rich memory, melody and best words,
urgent fire riding sun, moon and red dust,
a hat wearing big momma with an iowa ph.d.
Poet of solid songs, cotton fields and Mississippi gumbo,
messenger of our south, Rising.
if truth be liberated, her work navigated the student's spirit in
us.
she left literature, smiles, and ironwood wisdom.
she prepared us to see Black Earth.
daylight at the river's edge always
ready to extinguish square curves and invisible scars.
she was our railroad,
southwind and portrait,
our earth fed tree, soul rooted and able,
clearly a spirited dancer in a land not expecting us to
rise.

For Margaret Walker Alexander, 1915 -1998

When 21 is More Than A Number

we all knew them,
they were our children, Chicago's brightmoments.
their deaths stole our hearts   and
tragically touched a nation.
their memory occupies our dreams,
our waking minutes and the
seconds of our deep contemplations.
we are now in the rough tomorrows
of pain, outrage and reordering.

these young people,
these daughters and sons,
these developing geniuses at the
apex of their calling
would demand a renewed commitment
to smiles, safe territory and the noticing of simple pleasures:
grass, sun, the unhurried walk of the elderly,
the magical laughter of the innocent,
dancing to the melodies of love,
embracing the education of young seekers,
the taste of fresh grapes, watermelon, peaches and water.

as unthinkable as it seems today
we remain the wind and lake of their missed lives,
we are the answers to their unasked questions,
we are the on-goings, get-ups and critical yeses of future days,
we are the westside/southside of their walked streets,
we are the souls, spirits, and source of their beginnings.
do not render their lives irrelevant
they would want us to magnify the
alphabet enlightening the tongues of children.

For the 21 young people who perished in the E2 fire in Chicago on
February 17, 2003

Eighty-three is a Wise Number

The weather does not age, it
changes
bringing peach and hurricane,
water
and sun for planting, walking
and smiles
extending people to long life,
maybe.

I've grown up in your magic,
shadows and words,
I've seen you manage pens,
paper, poor eyesight and gift
giving.
I've measured the recent dip in
your walk,
noting the way the wind leans
you into its current
and I worry.

What if I'm not there to catch
your arm
to gently steer you away from a
fall, missed step
or from harm's way

but you've always been your
own clock
and as the seasons disappear
and rise
you know exactly what time it
is,
beating the beat in storms not
of your making.

for Gwendolyn Brooks at 83

Gwendolyn Brooks Illinois State Library: The Naming, June 6, 2003

your ancestry is book country,
able bones crossing the atlantic ocean to discover
white pages, protein and protégé in the midland.

in my first days of learning I remember eyeglasses that joined
    your smile.
I recall your fingers, long, thin, delicately brown and touchable,
suited for turning book pages, appropriate for ink sculpturing
    on paper.
fingers connected to memory, a people, a culture,
    Chicago and this state.
using the language of 47th street, Springfield and Cambridge,
    your poetry
silences us with its narrative love-songs, ripe-sources
    and bone-truths.
poems that governed the weather, invented eyes the colors
    of wheat, sky, coal,
cabbage, soybeans and yes, creating images out of empty
    pockets and kitchenettes.
art that reversed massacred thought, healthy words renouncing
ignorance, providing a
landscape of glorious literature
emphasizing lineage, liberty and validation.
your discourse is of children, the four seasons:
poetry that deciphers myths.
your writing: the impulse to arrive at meaning, life-ringing
    idioms, bright-calm
all accenting wisdom that affirmed in us the kindness
    of your grand spirit,
the friendliness of ideas, melodies and soap operas,
of water, sun and clean fire. your language is of
the necessity of carrot juice, broccoli and fattening chocolate,
of solitude, good pens and fine paper,
the labor of writers, poets, musicians and under-fed artists,

of librarians, libraries, books and break-even bookstores,
the support of printers, editors and struggling book publishers,
of book festivals, newspapers, magazines and twice-a-year
    quarterlies,
the requirement of contemplation, dialogue with others
    and reading on trains,
of legislators thinking outside the prism of dark suits
    and half-stories.

our ancestry is book country and rich earth,
galloping souls and skillful deal makers.
we are becoming the portrait of your right words.

Word Founder

he who takes the notes and
lost pages of the bitterly grounded,
he who files the failed memories
of the physically and psychologically beaten,
culturally enslaved and misrepresented billions;

he who documents the life stories of the people
whose voices are compromised each millisecond
of each second of each day
from sun high to moon light—
a people whose loud and clear whispers,
screamed and heartfelt autobiographies
bounce off the muted ears of a corrupted scholarship;

he who comprehends the unique power of storytelling
and intimately interprets concepts
that voice a people's narratives
especially the lifelines of Africans whose saneness
was stolen, hijacked and colonialized
by Euro-Americans disguised as authorities,
saviors and, of course, revelation, as well as, the blessed
descendents of the descendents who created civilization,
popcorn, rubber bands, the wheel and something called race
and measured intelligence;
he is welcomed Word Founder.

to you—meticulous researcher,
attentive listener and prudent recorder—
we say, yes.   To your mind's eye,
your calm commitment, authenticity;
love of truth,
we, the beneficiaries of your peaceful calling,
singular oeuvre and numerous struggles
say, yes.   To you, our able sage and seer—
original, rooted and serious educator,
a mountain of optimism and faith,

a hurricane of energy, spirit and Black love,
a volcano whose fire has quieted and is rested
let the chorus sing
yes—ashe,
yes—ashe,
yes—ashe,
ashe, ashe, ashe.

For Jacob H. Carruthers (1930-2004)

Water

we are the stories we are told,
they create boundaries in our voices.
we answer to names that are not ours,
African bones are buried on foreign soil and
our children are taught by people who do not
love them.

enter the mountain of truth
enter the rain drops of wisdom
enter the valley of right voices
enter the waves on the dark sea
enter the geography of a new continent
enter the enlightenment of Black
enter the quality of first thought.

he arrived in June, left in February
he farmed and fished for eighty nine years.
he created circles, mutual light
hands that touched prayer,
words that reordered memory,
ancestral stories of The Black Messiah,
he started a nation of believers who believed in themselves.

they say he is resting in Beulah Land.

For Jaramogi Abebe Agyeman
First Holy Patriarch
Pan African Orthodox Christian Church
August 1, 2003

The Sea in Your Language

She came to Urbana loving literature
stayed to start a movement among wheat, soybeans & vacant
  smiles
words always precede battle and battery
even where the language is not broken, torn or wanting.
Amidst the English-English you do not disappoint.
Revelation: its rough being a woman, black, slim, immaculate
with a brain as quick as fire in their tongue and ours.

Radical surgery allowed you to walk away from fear
making you incapable of treachery or grinning rhetoric.
Words matter. Some cut like big Willie's razor, bloodless.
others come deceptively like Vietnamese art, long history, short
  notice.
Twenty years of working in white shadows
qualifies you for a double zero preceding your name.
Your memory is of banished bones and promises.

Did I say she is the sea in you and me, and
morning tulips, red spirits, rainbow colors. Wow!
Our kind of woman. Running buddy, Sister, Genuine.
Announce her as valuable earth, hatwearer with a killer smile.

For Sandra Gibbs
November 20, 1999

Heart Work

Art has its own answers and name,
has beauty, insight and great questions too.
the poem is the unheard inquiry,
a foreign language in English and off rhyme
torturously taught by P.E. teachers
to a population bred on commercials and war games,
where the loud aesthetic is the nation's weapon
limited only by the zeros on its dollar bills.
You go substratum to decipher
the secrets of poets, musicians and hand painters.
Poetry has blanketed your heart and
your heart is like that of "Lincoln West," "Strong Men" and
"Mollie Means"
running alone on A Street in Bronzeville and Southern back
roads.

For the Teachers of Poetry

Useni

at 70 he still collects medals
for the ten minute mile he runs with a soft smile,
knowing he is one of three
in his age class in the race
who can
beat the sixty and under upstarts
who think that he is younger
than he claims.
reluctantly they eat his dust
and marvel at the beauty of his wife,
not aware of his real life
as poet.
tradition has it that most poets
have good looking women close by.
it is part of their job description.
yet, this useni man
does have a respectable career
where young men call him baba,
study his books and
quietly listen to the rhythms of his words,
seeking insight into his deep humanity
and running secrets.
i fail to inform you that this poet
is in league with Baraka, Wilson, Hansberry,
Hughes, and Ted Ward in capturing our
endless souls for the stage.

He is our anticipation,
life with an open heart of affirmations,
my love for him is earth grown,
spirited and brotherfed
we are wondrous of his gifts, longevity, and bad eating habits.

For Useni Eugene Perkins on his seventieth birthday
September 13, 2003

Aunt Mayme

there was this distant desert a half century away,
on the negro door to "jew town" at chicago's 14th and hastings,
on a one house street with a broom factory on the corner,
where stood a home, with walk over stairs connecting sidewalk
to hope,
where summers and other drop-off times were spent
with a loving aunt, many children and an uncle
larger than doorways named jesse james.
he wore guns, had a majestic smile on a large
bald head. he adored his family and worked all the time.

our days were spent collecting metal and saleable junk
in secure alleys where work was not begging for jobs
but inventing employment, making do with ideas and nothing.
knowing that if everything is everything,
then nothing is nothing.
except we, my sister and I, had aunt mayme for precious
moments with uncle jesse who worked all the time.

during summers and some autumns at irregular
drop-offs, my sister and I received uncommon love,
full meals, deep warmth and learned the location of family
from aunt mayme, a host of first cousins
and that giant of a black man with guns,
a winning and intelligent smile,
pre-MJ bald head
with promises and safety in his eyes.

On her 75th birthday, February 1, 2003

Duke

was it Duke Ellington
who said that
music was his mistress?
she musta been
fine
wore red, read poetry and prose
could swing naturally,
danced a lot and didn't need
too much sleep.

Tee One in a Complex World

this woman
does good when good is unnoticeable or advertised,
she carries rocks to the dams of beavers,
writes memorandum of possibilities for single mothers,
vows publicly for the security of children,
hears the prophets' voices from the roots of oak trees,
would give you her leg
if she didn't have to walk.

this woman
can read a smile in evil,
studies the earth's waterfalls,
understands iambic pentameter,
reads the sacred texts of Africa and Israel,
she sings the lyrics of Shirley Horn
while monitoring the intricate speech of her progeny
who converses in coded alphabet and colors.

her kisses are climactic
an oral lover who has a fondness for carrot juice.
she memorizes the sensitive nerves of her men and
attends to the feet of the difficult musician on her block.
her decisive word to him was no
as she prepared to travel foreign waters
to kiss new trees.

this woman is artful earth opening for the seeds awaiting her.

Maya: We Honor Our Own

your voice bridged genre,
in concert with Malcolm, Killens, Baldwin and Brooks
it matured us,
stamped us to ourselves,
impelled a recognition that had been contradicted
by priest and anthropologist,
by banker and architect.

your voice, able, harmonious and emphatic,
willfully free and angular
dared to confront our fears,
invade our interiors and weak utterances.
Maya, a wandering call back,
our precise reminder.
no longer a test pilot,
welcome
poet who can boogie-down.
you are among the last of the great trees,
high questioner, master wordgiver and witness.
you've paid our dues,
there is no copy, clown or apology here.

we find home in your presence.

For Maya Angelou, Howard University – Heart's Day 2004

45

For R. Kelly

if you have daughters?
how you gointa
protect them
from the somebodies
just like you?

Wynton

that boy musta been listenin to Pops
he plays trumpet real good
just like Satchmo when he hot,
my grandfather announced.
I agreed and more.

the trumpet seems like it is
sewn to his lips
cause he plays like
Sterling Brown reading his poems.
and we all know poetry comes from God.

For Wynton Marsalis

Butt for Sale: The Gateway to Factualization

rising quickly under the umbrella of scholar extraordinaire
professor greats, dr. heavy loose greats, aka jump greats to
close associates, friends and spelling buddies, recently of yale,
cornell, duke and now residing permanently at the cambridge
of America.

rising energetically to the undeniable
challenge of Black-Blackness
and african centered ideas running amuck
from uncertified upstarts,
captain greats, the queen of rebuttal, designated hit man,
the protector of rap & sap, the answerer to out
of order negroes,
honorary defender of the forgotten misogynist 2 live crew,
rappers who wouldn't recognize a syllable that was pro-Black
women if it bit their tongues as they struggled against the devil
to scream money without the B____, F____ & N____ words
that decorate & inflate their male insightfulness.

now, rising cleverly on the western horizon super scholar for
hire, wordsmith on the negro-right, chairperson
and proclaimer of white truths, coming like a dull
razor cutting clear speech, dr. jump, the last word, eloquently
ascending from the lower middle east-side of Manhattan
where real men are made and turned-out with the frequency of
run away children forced into prostitution, comes the most
sought after H.N.I.C.[1] the world has known since the
unquestioned rhyme, reason & puppetry of the marvelous
stepin fetchit, is dr. heavy loose greats.

climbing ruthlessly and uninhibited on the op-ed pages of
"All the News That's Fit to Print"[2] is professor *jump*
who is crowned prince of B for Black studies, Black with an
enlarged A, as in anti-African thought, dr. greats is in
the house residing as the advocate of white, Zionist and

wahhabist il-liberal ideas of advanced thought. professor
greats, the respected expert on everything colored, negro,
Black, African, afro-American, brown, unwhite, mulatto and
coon is the gifted yes-sir-boss of the new century.

give him his due as he rises against the sun, sons and
daughters blessed by the sun who dared to question the
illegality and brutality of enslavement, dare to examine ideas
unsanctioned or confirmed
by the official canonicals, dare to fight acts that have
disfigured Black minds and bodies:
acts & ideas that produced the unspoken,
under-studied or acknowledged holocaust
of the African middle passage and beyond.

dr. greats rising happily and comfortably against the dark
people who battle brain mismanagement hourly,
rising strategically with a clown's grin to be anointed by
"all the news that's fit to print," "the new yorker" and cambridge
of the east as authentic and accredited Black, afro-American
and authority on watermelon seed spitting.

professor greats is on board to uncover the "anti-white,"
"anti-jewish," therefore ungodly, unrighteous conspiracy of
Blacks who think. he and his assistants are on a
mission to uproot the "Black demagogues" and
"pseudo-scholars"
who must be neutralized, must be cut off at the knees,
as in kneel niggers; must be whited-out. dr. greats, one among
many who are maid boys and economically armed to clean
the corridors of Black/African intrusion once and forever.

greaterman ascending in perfect pitch, possessing a technical
magnetism and imagination, the newest star of negro studies,
the honorary european of the left, right and center.
the corrector, the yellow highlighter for the west, untouched by
ancestor worship, shoddy scholarship and rib eating contests.

greaterman running uncensored and alive, last seen
at cambridge mini lecturing to wide eyed future
directors of M16, CIA and the ghost of viking
barbarians in dark suits all learning close textual
reading and listening. we have greaterman joyously jumping
to the beat of alien women in heat and skipping to the polka
of white rulership demanding confirmed articulations
of former slaves.

greaterman, the clarence thomas of modern grantsmanship,
is able to leap long sentences in simple utterances, able
to survey African civilizations in a brief phase, able to
disarm and dismantle young scholars with a mere glance and
promises of book contracts, able to terrorize untenured
assistant professors in unmusical prose, collaborated by the
primary sources on the back of cereal boxes as he films the
entire continent of Africa and its people in a tee-shirt.

dr. heavy loose greats, aka jump, reborn on the
yes plantation of sambo universality, is now the
unquestioned, unchallenged sovereign on the negro.
he plays daily and deadly in the legitimate journals,
magazines, newspapers, broadcasts, colleges and courts
of the euro-world.
yet and yet,
jumperman is unwelcomed in the eyes
of Black children and incarcerated boymen,
is forbidden to eat at the table
of African mothers & fathers who
anticipate the horror and prepare for the cowardly carnage
that certified niggers do
yielding white hatchets,
dripping Black blood.

Notes
[1]Head Negro In Charge
[2]see Op-Ed page, *New York Times*, July 20, 1992

What We Don't Know

how do full time talkers,
"human rights" organizers & spokes persons who
have never known employment,
never dirtied their hands at
carpentry, garbage pick-up, nursing,
window cleaning, plumbing or
butchering fried chicken that widens their waist-lines
live so well?

Should they not share the secrets of the militant
unemployed who change town cars yearly,
vacation in exclusive communities,
demand private planes and sex partners,
solicit front-row seats at fights,
super bowls, all star games,
Las Vegas openings' and pork chop eating roasts?

the large perception is that we are
led by men (& a few women) who bathe in integrity,
who are believed to be walking in the footsteps of Malcolm,
Martin, Medgar and Parks,
yet they tailor their suits and ideas,
bishop over failing colleges and victim-talk,
pop-up for cameras and microphones
as perfectionist in the art of one-liners and people politics
strategically misusing the race card.

how do full time God talkers
become millionaires in America
be they Christian, Jews or Muslim?
what we don't know is
some bodies in the moments & minutes
of daylight, after hours and blinking eyes
must be
in the capital and corporate offices of money
making side deals with the devil.

For the Consideration of Poets

where is the poetry of resistance,
        the poetry of honorable defiance
unafraid of lies from career politicians and business men,
not respectful of journalist who write
official speak void of educated thought
without double search or sub surface questions
that war talk demands?
where is the poetry of doubt and suspicion
not in the service of the state, bishops and priests,
not in the service of beautiful people and late night promises,
not in the services of influence, incompetence and academic
        clown talk?

III

A Poet's Handbook

A Poet's Handbook

You may not be able to earn a living exclusively as a poet or writer, but if you persist, work hard and nurture your talent; it is almost guaranteed that you will earn a life. To choose to be a "poet" as a professional endeavor is not very high on the preferred or most lucrative career path in our nation, therefore as a poet, you must adhere to a few standard and not so standard rules.

———————

Poetry will not stop or delay wars, will not erase rape
       from the landscape,
will not cease murder or eliminate poverty, hunger or
excruciating fear. Poems do not command armies, run
school systems or manage money. Poetry is not
intimately involved in the education of psychologists,
physicians or smiling politicians.

in this universe
the magic   the beauty   the willful art of explaining
the world & you;
the timeless   the unread   the unstoppable fixation
with language & ideas;
the visionary   the satisfiable equalizer screaming for
the vitality of dreams   interrupting false calm
demanding fairness and a new   new world are the
poets and their poems.

Poetry is the wellspring of tradition, the bleeding
connector to yesterdays and the free passport to futures.
Poems bind people to language, link generations to
each other and introduce cultures to cultures.
Poetry, if given the eye and ear, can bring memories,
issue in laughter, rain in beauty and cure ignorance.
Language in the context of the working poem can
raise the mindset of entire civilizations, speak to two

year olds and render some of us wise.
To be touched by living poetry can only make us
    better people.
The determined force of any age is the poem, old as
ideas and as lifegiving as active lovers. A part of any
answer is in the rhythm of the people; their heartbeat
comes urgently in two universal forms, music and poetry.
for the reader   for the quiet seeker
for the many willing to sacrifice one syllable
mumblings and easy conclusions
poetry
can be that gigantic river
that allows one to recognize
in the circle of fire
the center of life.

One

Learn to "run toward fear." Understand that—even with the emergence of performance poetry and poetry slams and the increasing number of individuals who profess to be poets—few people actually read poetry. Understand that although small-minded individuals rule the world, it is always right to question, challenge and hold them accountable for their actions.

Two

Think about, read, and study more poetry than you write.

Three

Repeat number two.

Four

Minimize the praise given to your poetry from parents, friends, lovers, siblings, spouses, running buddies, cheerleading squads, creditors and former lovers.

Five

Read and study good poetry from all cultures and, if possible, try to talk to poets whose work you respect and enjoy. However, be realistic about what to expect from them. Most poets are too busy talking to themselves and may not always hear the whispers from the next generation of poets.

Six

Do not anticipate informed or knowledgeable guidance on the craft of poetics from family, friends, lovers, scout troop leaders or strangers looking for a handout.

Seven

Never give up on love, children and good poetry. Immerse yourself in the work of a poet that you admire. Read every poem that he or she has published, keeping a careful eye on his or her growth line. Examine their work for instruction rather than for imitation. Read about the lives of poets and writers from publications like *Poets and Writers, Black Issues Book Review, QBR: The Black Book Review* and *The Writer's Chronicle*.

Eight

Upon people discovering your secret life as a poet, get accustomed to them asking, often with little subtlety, "Okay, but what do you do for a living?"

Nine

Prepare yourself to be able to make a living in many professions, such as: movie popcorn maker, clown, grocery bagger, after-hour escort, bookstore clerk, nanny's assistant and highway ticket toll-booth money-taker, naturally these are temporary jobs that require little thought as you think mainly about making poems.

Ten

Write your truth and you will seldom have writers' block. Always carry a pen and notebook with you in order to catch the unusual comments, conversations, lies, slogans and picturesque words that pepper everyday speech of everyday people.

Eleven

Most people think that they can write poetry. Many of them are right and need encouragement.

Twelve

If you are seeking immediate success, write poems that only critics, other poets and their dogs understand. If you write lies well individuals, politicians, "beautiful" people, institutions and foundations will throw grants and favors at you. Of course, liars rule in politics, religion, and business, but do not necessarily make good poets.

Thirteen

In the beginning, middle and late years of your writing career, learn to live on minimal financial resources or marry well (translation: anybody with a job, an understanding of commitment and preferably a person who doesn't talk too much).

Fourteen

Study music, the closest art to poetry, especially the music of great Black jazz, blues, and reggae musicians. Study the music of indigenous peoples of all lands.

Fifteen

Visit other cultures. Study their laughter and language, as well as, the reasons they don't like Americans.

Sixteen

Never give up on love, children, good poetry, writing and music. The best poets are masters at understatement and language efficiency—knowing what words to use and not to use. The best poets are able to cut the fat from each line and are masters at haiku. Good poetry inches along and does not travel at the speed of antelopes.

Seventeen

Complete an undergraduate program (in your selected field of interest) with the awareness that in today's economic climate an undergraduate degree is equivalent to a trade union card, and is not a bad thing to have if you actually learned something beneficial about life, poetry, literature, politics and economics.

Closely study the world of publishing. It is a complicated and very corporate business. I recommend that you start by reading a few books about publishing. *The Business of Books* by Andre Schiffrin, *Book Business* by Jason Epstein, and *The Practical Writer* edited by Eiben and Gannon are all strong introductions into the publishing business. Read as many of the magazines and journals pertaining to the book business and writing as you are able: *Publishers Weekly, Black Issues Book Review* (BIBR), *QBR: The Black Book Review,* and the *Literary Market Place* (which can be found at most main branches of the public library, it represents a major resource for editors, printers, publishers, agents and awards). Read *Callaloo, Brilliant Corners, African American Review, Writer's Digest, The American Poetry Review, Poetry, Ruminator, Bloomsbury Review, The New York Review of Books, African Voices, Mosaic, Poets and Writers* and *The Writer's Chronicle* and the many quarterlies issued from university presses from across the country. Read the book sections of *The New York Times, The Washington Post, Los Angeles Times, The Chicago Tribune, The Village Voice, Essence Magazine* and your local newspaper. Whenever possible attend book festivals, writer conferences and book events. Check out C-SPAN, especially Book TV on C-SPAN2 each weekend. Finally, always support your independent booksellers.

Eighteen

Honor and nurture the innocence of children, first that of your own children and then of others. Their laughter—which is free, inspiring, and contagious— is the closest act of pure joy that is available on earth. Remember most children love hearing good poetry. Introduce children, early and often, to poetry and good literature rather than television and fast food.

Nineteen

One activity that is free, joyful and life-giving is a simple walk in the woods. The appreciation of nature; to enjoy its benefits will, on occasion, require that you leave large urban areas and learn to breathe, walk, and stretch (for the uninformed this is the beginning of yoga). Healthy poets write healthy poems. Give your body at least an hour a day of exercise, prayer or meditation, and strength training. Read and eat nutritiously, both require some study. Poetry should not cause harm; poetry should, as much as possible, be part of preventative health; that is healthy poetry.

Twenty

Peace is more than a 1960's era concern or aspiration. While many write about the atrocities and consequences of war and violence, most poets are not advocates of war or violence. They are, but for a few exceptions, deeply into life and love. Thinking, acting and writing peacefully should be a goal. Question everything, especially the anti-people uses of the World Bank, International Monetary Fund, World Trade Organization and the North American Free Trade Agreement. The best poets find peace in themselves and work incessantly to find it in others, their surroundings, and on more than one occasion write poems about the necessity and possibility of a world at peace.

Twenty-one

Keep an active library card. An excellent free library in a poet's community is the best medicine for neutralizing ignorance. Free public libraries are also good environments in which to write if one doesn't have a quiet home in which to work. Most of all, libraries represent vast possibilities for acquiring knowledge; and libraries are anti-ignorance.

Twenty-two

Writing is revision. If you work at the craft of writing it will require extensive revision and rewriting. The only time that the first, second or even third draft of a poem is acceptable is when you are writing for church bulletins and weekly racing forms.

Twenty-three

Never give up on love, children, good poetry, writing, music and visual art. Own a good dictionary and thesaurus. A good poetry dictionary is also a necessity. I recommend *The Poetry Dictionary* by John Drury.

Twenty-four

Circulate your work to publications that publish poetry and creative writing. And when you do, expect to receive rejections—most coming from small journals and magazines, university presses, white main-stream book publishers, amateur football teams, high school swimming squads, the opposite sex, the same sex, people with money, critics, editors, failed poets who are now critics, professors and protectors of free enterprise (whatever that is?).

Twenty-five

Remember, contrary to the examples of Robert Lowell, Sylvia Plath, Ernest Hemingway, John Berryman, Anne Sexton and others in the Western canon, suicide or what Joyce Carol Oates called "self-murder" is not the norm. In fact, killing one's self is anti-poetry. Find a writing community that nurtures and encourages the creative life-force and breath-cycle of poetry and literature that is in all of us. A poet may write alone but should not be alone.

Twenty-six

Study all forms of poetry. Only then will you realize how not to write poetry. There are profound differences between academic formal verse and free verse, between accentual meter and un-metered verse.

Twenty-seven

Limit your association with malls, Hummer2, rah-rah crowds, alcohol and drugs, people who find life in talking about others, people who have never worked with their hands, people who think that poetry writing is done by others and people who hate books.

Twenty-eight

Travel. Get out of your personal space. Walk beyond your street, learn another language, seek other communities of poets and writers, communicate with artists outside of your discipline, always keep copious notes, learn to smile naturally and often. Life is short, hang on to every precious moment. Do not be afraid of a spiritual or religious life force. Study various spiritual paths, always keeping in mind that good poetry often comes from the least expected of us and often in the worse of times.

Twenty-nine

Seek perfection in the writing of poetry, recognizing that perfection in any art is a journey and requires arduous preparation, single-minded focus, an open and nourished mind and a love for the art and craft of poetry writing that few outside of the family of poets or community of artist comprehend.

Thirty

Never give up in love, children, good poetry, writing, music, visual art and theater. Visit other creative communities. How did John Coltrane create? What drove the art of Romare Bearden and Elizabeth Catlett? What is the source that produces the literature of Toni Morrison, Walter Mosley, bell hooks, Richard Wright and Ishmael Reed? What motivates Amiri Baraka?

Thirty-one

Write each day with an understanding that early drafts of your poems may not be ready for publication or public readings. The requirements for writing good and publishable poetry are cemented in the ability of poets to effectively revise and rework or reorder their ideas into poems that shine and jump off the page like a baby's smile after a feeding.

Thirty-two

Good does exist in the world. However, Western artists of all persuasions are often pessimistic and driven to the dark side of life. A sea change is needed. One cannot find that which is good, correct or just and write about such concepts if one is drugged-up, high only on one's self, running with the distress of the world or raised only on fast foods, commercial culture and wolves in human form.

Thirty-three

The best poets are people persons. They study women, study men and visit their places of comfort, such as beauty shops, barber shops, work spaces and centers of worship. They listen to conversations, politics, jokes, gossip and the deep concerns of the people they write about. They are able to filter noise from content, are not afraid of beauty or ugliness. They are keenly aware of the sonnets of Gwendolyn Brooks and the narrative poems of Sterling A. Brown and Robert Hayden.

Thirty-four

Remain skeptical of presidents, secretaries of state, secretaries of defense, national security advisors, national, state and local politicians, most clergy, 95% of what is broadcast on A.M. and F.M. radio, 96% of all television, 85% of the world-wide web, most newspapers and magazines, 100% of gossip from all cultures. Remember to sleep lightly, question in detail all authority (especially that which is funded from our taxes) and question men and women who carry guns for a living.

Thirty-five

Never give up on love, children, good poetry, writing, music, visual art, theater and dance. Find fresh language, and avoid clichés in the same manner as you would avoid bad food and bad breath. Believe in art. Gwendolyn Brooks writes that "Art hurts. Art urges voyages."

Thirty-six

Poets who have redefined the art of poetry writing and most likely will not be taught in the academy, appear on recommended reading lists and are not frequently anthologized are many. They, the unsung poets, need to be glued to your conscience like seeds to earth if you wish to grow and experience the wealth of great poetry that exists in the world. Just to get you started, I've developed a list of contemporary poets and writers whose works you may want to incorporate into your own library. Among the familiar names, I've also included some of these lesser-known poets and voices:

Gwendolyn Brooks, Amiri Baraka, Mari Evans, Julia Fields, Langston Hughes, Frank Marshall Davis, Margaret Walker, Robert Hayden, Jayne Cortez, June

Jordan, Melvin B. Tolson, Lucille Clifton, Sterling A. Brown, Daniel Berrigan, Alice Walker, Samuel Allen, Ishmael Reed, Mahmoud Darwish, Muriel Rukeyser, A.B. Spellman, Leopold Sedar Senghor, Audre Lorde, Sterling D. Plumpp, Maya Angelou, Claude McKay, Sonia Sanchez, Kamau Brathwaite, Wendell Berry, Nikky Finney, Dudley Randall, Sascha Feinstein, Larry Neal, Naomi Long Madgett, Lisel Mueller, E. Ethelbert Miller, Kalamu ya Salaam, Ana Castillo, Octavio Paz, Aime Cesaire, Pablo Neruda, Eugene Redmond, Charles Simic, Henry Dumas, Joy Harjo, Kevin Stein, Adrienne Rich, Angela Jackson, Robert Bly, Sandra Cisneros, Miguel Algarin, Ruth Garnett, Carl Sandburg, Nikki Giovanni, Quincy Troupe, Carolyn M. Rodgers, Etheridge Knight, Marvin Bell, Billy Collins, Wanda Coleman, Michael S. Harper, Fred Hord, Tony Medina, Shirley Anne Williams, Keorapetse Kgositsile, Luis Rodriguez, Yusef Komunyakaa, Ntozake Shange, Clarence Major, Al Young, Rita Dove, Bob Kaufman, Quraysh Ali Lansana, Yehuda Amichai, Toi Derricotte, Reginald Gibbons, Edward Hirsch, Lawrence Ferlinghetti, Dolores Kendrick, Elizabeth Alexander, Brian Gilmore, Michael Anania, G.E. Murray, D.H. Melhem, Nicolas Guillen, Cornelius Eady, Dennis Brutus, Useni Eugene Perkins, Alvin Aubert, Carlos Cumpian, Li-Young Lee, Martin Espada, Gwendolyn Mitchell, Walt Whitman, Jessica Care Moore, Wole Soyinka, Jerry W. Ward Jr., Keith Gilyard, David Hernandez, Gerald Stern, Askia M. Toure, Pinky Gordon Lane, Kevin Powell, Anjail Rashida Ahmad, Harryette Mullen, Asha Bendele, Everett Hoagland, Afaa Micheal Weaver, Natasha Trethewey, Lamont B. Steptoe, Jabari Asim, Estella Conwill Majozo, Ai, Kelly Norman Ellis, Julie Parson-Nesbitt, Derek Walcot, Yeugeny Yeutushanko, Thomas Lux, Sam Greenlee, Kevin Young, Tyhimba Jess, Opal Moore, Haki R. Madhubuti and those who have influenced you not listed here.

Thirty-seven

Never give up on love, children, good poetry, writing, music, visual art, theatre, dance, books and the power of "Art" to transform and make progressively whole the most backward of people and those disguised as human beings. Verbal Art is a universal art and is the most democratic of Arts. The heart and soul of a poet is the love of reading, writing and the developmental possibilities of Art.

Thirty-eight

The highest mandate a poet has (other than writing the strongest poems that she or he is capable of) is to be in the vanguard with others in the pursuit of freedom and justice for all. The next mandate is to write in the tradition of poets like Gwendolyn Brooks, Robert Bly, Adrienne Rich and Amiri Baraka all of whom have been 24/7 foot soldiers/street fighters for peace and a decent life for all. Their lives have been about creating poetry and art for "people sake" rather than only for "art sake."

Thirty-nine

Poets must be able to, at any given time, run toward fear against the bomb users, greed promoters, career politicians, corporate plastic makers, armies of the money-makers, pleasure-over-principle advocates, proponents of artificial food. Poets must be acutely aware of "fame" which is like a flame in the brain and will cut serious writing potential by 85% and turn most of the poets it consumes into game show participants who seek the confidence of Whoopi Goldberg, Snoop Dogg and other cultural embarrassments.

Forty

Write the poems you want to read, hopefully with moral vision and clarity that will inspire all of us to want to read and write poems. Poets are not perfect, however, most of the best have in them the unique capacity to create great poems, and thus constructing a statement about "art" and life that, in a few critical words, can help us face our worse fears and hopefully make this world a better place for our children and poetry. Finally, always question your own heart and be free enough to look into the eyes a child with a secure and welcoming smile that affirms— "you can do this too."